FETCH

By

Yvonne Hamilton

Fetch an act of going for something and then bringing it back: *he thought the best part of the fetch was wrestling over the stick*

New Oxford Dictionary of English

impspired@gmail.com

Artwork by Yvonne Hamilton

ISBN: 978-1-915819-13-0

To celebrate a time when children and dogs were free to wander.

A magical time that cannot be brought back

OTHER TITLES BY IMPSPIRED

Adele and Tom –
by Chella Courington

Periodic Stories Vol. 4 -
by Jim Bates

Inferno –
by Nicolas D. Sampson

The River -
by Theresa C. Gaynord

Echoes –
by Gordon Ferris

Curiosity –
by Geraldine Fleming

Incandescence –
by Mehreen Ahmed

INTRODUCTION

It was only when she was requested by her daughter-in-law to write a "This Is Your Life" type speech for one of her son's major birthdays that Yvonne Hamilton began to realize how carefree and happy her childhood had been. As she worked through the speech she saw that a number of dogs had played a significant role in the childhood she had shared first with her brother, then later with her children.

With the birthday safely over, she commenced recording her Dog Stories so that the childhood of the past would be remembered and understood by those coming after her. The arrival of Covid, isolating children from their friends, their school mates and even members of extended family, was in such stark contrast to the life Yvonne had known that she started to toy with recording her memories in a more permanent form.

ACKNOWLEDGEMENTS

Though I had written many of the stories before I joined North Coast Writers, it is thanks to the members of that group that I was encouraged to share my efforts, gaining the confidence to believe that all was possible.

Thanks also to Margaret Roberts and William Wilson for advice and support.

I am most grateful to Mary Farrell of North Coast Writers, one of the many interest groups within Causeway u3a, and Steve Cawte at Impspired Press who made the possible a reality.

Finally, I say 'thank you' to - and for - all the dogs that have crossed my path and enriched my life.

No Life is complete without a dog, writes Gerald Durrell. In this collection of stories, the Author introduces us to dogs of all breeds, shapes and sizes while celebrating their limitless affection and loyalty. In its pages you will find the canine joy of tail-wagging dogs, dogs who tumble and play with golf balls, sticks and rubber rings, dogs who escape with glee, but above all, dogs who were allowed to expand their individual personalities in a world where they knew they were safe and loved. These stories tell us as much about the Narrator as the dogs. She shared her world with them showing kindness and an open heart. In return, they gave back to her a rich tapestry of memories. Sharing these, a reader feels their core warming and their face smiling.

The accompanying artwork, drawn by the author herself, captures the uniqueness and charm of each dog. You know these images were drawn with affectionate, and sometimes mischievous, brush strokes. These are dogs you want to reach out and stroke on the page.

Written in a charming, distinctive voice, these tales evoke a different time. Yvonne Hamilton calls it 'a time when children and dogs were free to wander, a magical time which cannot be brought back'. In our increasingly busy and conscripted lives, we look back poignantly at this era. These stories help soothe the stresses of our modern living, and remind us of what is truly of value in our lives - mutual love, respect and tolerance.

Mary Farrell is an Author who co-ordinates three Creative Writing Groups in Northern Ireland. She is also the Creative Writing Facilitator for Impspired Press.

CONTENTS

SCAMP

The very first dog

For the most of my life a dog has featured. From the time when my mother placed me in the playpen and the family Airedale jumped in to keep me company and guard over me, till I decided that it would be unkind to commit to another dog in the assumption that it would out last me.

I cannot claim to remember Karl, the Airedale, though his existence is confirmed in family photos, but he must have been quite an exceptional animal when he was allowed, indeed encouraged, to share a play-pen with a toddler.

The first dog that I remember was called Daisy, a long-haired brown and white Lassie type Collie that belonged on my maternal Grandmother's farm at the foot of a mountain on the edge of a bog in the south of Ireland. The farm was almost self-sufficient with a little of everything except sheep. For some reason that never was explained to me the dog shared its name with my mother's sister so, to ensure that we knew which Daisy was being addressed or discussed, the dog became Daisydog.

For the month of July every year my brother and I joined a cousin of the same age for a holiday on the farm. Daisydog followed us round while we gathered eggs, fed hens, fetched the cows, climbed trees in the orchard, picked blackcurrants, saved the hay, carried in the turf and water, had countless adventures in the huge garden and the surrounding fields. We had chores that we were expected to do but, once these were accomplished, we were free to wander with the bog the only part of the farm from which we were banned.

My paternal grandfather died when I was still very young and my father explained his death to us assuring us that grandpa had been good and had gone to heaven so there was no more need for us to include him in our prayers because he was with God.

Later that year the news came that Daisydog had died. My brother was particularly affected by this as he adored Daisydog. He had been given a green and cream toy dog that he called Daisydog in an attempt by our parents to fulfil his burning wish for a dog of his own. Remembering my grandfather's death and the comfort the promise of a reunion in Heaven had been, I assured my brother that, though I knew he was very sad, he would see Daisydog again in Heaven so he should try not to cry. My ministering was overheard by my father, the oracle in religious matters, who explained to both of us that, in fact, dogs did not go to Heaven and we would not, therefore, see Daisydog again. This did nothing to dry up my brother's tears but led me to the conclusion that if there was no place for dogs in Heaven I had no interest in going there. I was seven.

The first dog that I considered 'Mine' arrived as a birthday present to my brother from an aunt who was ever there in the family circle. Looking back, even then I knew that there was an atmosphere attached to the appearance of that particular dog. My brother had been pleading for a dog with no success so the arrival of a pup for his birthday came as a huge surprise. When I say it was thrilling, that would be an understatement but I believe that it was a thrill not shared by my father. But my aunt, even though she was, and remained unmarried, knew something about managing the male of the species. Who could take a birthday present away from a seven-year-old boy!

My poor father never had a chance. He was completely outnumbered and outvoted by his family. To be fair he didn't put up a very strenuous fight and was gracious enough to throw himself enthusiastically into the debate over naming the new pup. Care needs to be taken to choose a name that would suit a short haired, short tailed, bouncing, brown bundle of fun that became Scamp.

Scamp was a mongrel. My brother knew enough about dogs to realise that some breeds carried more standing than others: he had heard of Great Danes, Alsatians and Airedales

He believed that it was important that he should know the breed of his dog when class mates enquired about it. He didn't exactly want to boast but thought his dog should have full and proper recognition. When he pressed my father and my aunt to tell him what breed Scamp was they were put in a rather difficult position. My father came up with what he thought was a very acceptable answer: Scamp was a pure-bred mongrel and that satisfied my brother – problem solved.

But my father realised that his joke had gone beyond the family when, a couple of weeks later, the principal of our primary school crossed the road to ask, with a twinkle in his eye, where my father had come across the dog as he understood that it was a very rare breed indeed. Matters had to be put right so we were set down and given a more truthful account of Scamp's possible ancestry. My brother went on to own a series of King Charles Spaniels but I remained faithful to the mongrel.

I have no idea how many breeds were represented in Scamp but he was well proportioned, healthy and extremely smart. He seemed to have no need to be taught but managed to pick things up all by himself. He became my mother's constant companion during school time and accompanied me at every opportunity outside school hours.

In those days, and I have a feeling that phrase may occur often in these stories, attitudes, opinions and ideas were very different allowing dogs to wander free from leads. There were very few cars so people either walked or cycled. Shops were scattered throughout the town so one did not have far to travel for groceries, milk and bread were delivered to houses regularly.

My mother used to do her grocery shopping by bicycle following a route that circled the town, parking the bicycle outside each shop while making her purchases. Sometimes Scamp managed to accompany her, barking and bouncing back and forth over the rear wheel. More often he was left at home.

However, he had a talent for escape and when my mother left him behind he frequently sneaked out and set off in pursuit, running, nose to ground till he either found the mistress who had deserted him or her bicycle parked outside a shop. Having found the bike he flopped down beside it, tail wagging, tongue lolling to await her return quite sure that she would be surprised and delighted to see him poised and ready to bark and bounce all the way home.

Just as he managed to sneak out when it suited him so also did he manage to sneak in. The biggest grocery store in the town was honoured by his presence on occasion. Back then the attitude to health and safety was much more relaxed. Dogs could visit shops. They were not exactly welcome but some shop keepers, even grocers, turned a blind eye particularly if the offending dog behaved and was the beloved pet of a valued customer.

In those days cheese came in huge wheels covered with a hard rind that was not eaten and had to be removed. Scamp discovered that these off cuts of cheese were dumped in a box in a corner near one of the two doors of the grocery store my mother frequented. Well, he loved cheese and was not going to let an opportunity like that pass. In he would sneak and gobble up what he could before the blind eye became all seeing and he was chased out to sit demurely beside the bike till the shopping was complete. But, though he smiled and wagged innocently at my mother when she joined him, he could not disguise the enormous hiccoughs that cheese always gave him. He bounced, barked and hiccoughed all the way home.

While he was tolerated in some shops there were two establishments where he was positively welcomed. At one end of the town the owners of a small shop that stocked a wonderful mix of articles for sale anything from a pencil to a cake loved to see Scamp. When he visited here he was given a seat, presented with a biscuit or piece of cake or a bun which he ate politely before continuing on his search for his mistress.

At the other end of the town Scamp ended his search at the butcher's shop where the owner treated him to titbits to help keep up his strength for the ongoing search. All donations were politely received with wagging tail.

Scamp was generous with his bouncing and barking. My mother was not the only one to be so honoured. Further along our street two teenage brothers shared a motorbike. Motorbikes were not a common sight in those days. It was a small one that made a high penetrating noise that could be heard from afar. Scamp could hear it long before it was audible to the human ear. If if he could manage it at all, charged after it bouncing and barking. The younger brother ignored the bouncing barking dog. With no reaction, Scamp lost interest and trotted home. However, the older brother was much more fun. When Scamp charged barking and bouncing he revved up, raced up the road shouting and kicking out as the dog chased him all the way home, ignoring all threats, kicks and curses… every time.

In some places dogs were never welcome the local cinema and our church. So, because of his habit of appearing behind us when we were positive that he had been secured in the house when we departed, he had to learn to go home. Now this was a lesson that did not come easily. He simply could not accept that he was not vital to the outing. I had to stretch my arm, point my finger, assume a VERY stern voice to say HOME, GO HOME. That was enough to stop him. A repeat of the command caused a half turn. On the third he turned in a homeward direction – head down, ears drooping, tail tucked in. He moved off, a picture of walking misery, casting glances over his shoulder just in case the finger no longer pointed or the arm had dropped. So, he never visited the cinema though he made it to the door a couple of times.

In those days church was much more formal than it is today. Children sat very quietly – no talking allowed and it was a source of great embarrassment if the penny destined for the collection plate fell by accident and rolled around on the wooden floor at any time during the service. Dogs never darkened the doors.

One Sunday morning when the church was full to overflowing my friends and I arrived just before the service started and had to sit at the front. We preferred less prominent seating. As the service was about to commence I became aware that one of the church officers was standing beside me and at the same time I felt something wet pressed at the side of my leg. There he was. Ears pricked up, tail wagging and tongue lolling as if to say 'Ah-ha. Here I am. Found you. Didn't I do well. You must be relieved to see me.'

The officer had followed Scamp to put him out but he possessed neither the long arm nor the pointing finger required for the job. So I had to march Scamp down the aisle, into the church grounds, point the finger etc. etc. Then scurried back to my seat at the front of the church while the whole congregation looked on. In retrospect, searching for a silver lining it has to be said that he didn't bark or bounce once!

In my youth many of the young folk of the town

spent much of their summer holidays at the outdoor swimming pool. Good weather or bad there we were swimming diving and chatting. Though Scamp loved to go ***to*** the pool he certainly did not approve of going ***into*** it. When we dived in, he circled the pool barking a warning about the dangers attached to getting into the water, bouncing and wagging in relief when we returned to dry land.

Sometimes, in the hope that it would stop him barking, one of the older boys would push him into the pool. Having done that, it was tempting to stay and laugh at Scamp as he scrambled out bedraggled, dripping and silent. If you yielded Scamp had his revenge. It is amazing how much water flies out of a wet shaking dog.

I was studying in the city when Scamp showed signs of declining. Each weekend when I came home I could see that there was less welcoming bounce till the day I returned and Scamp was gone. That was my first real experience of the death of a loved pet and I thought my heart would break.

Karl

The Dog I Failed

With the children gone from home my parents decided that it was time to enjoy their freedom without the responsibility of a pet so I was married and had a home of my own before another dog entered my life. It was decided that a dog was needed. We invested in a pedigree Alsatian which was selected from a litter owned by a local breeder. He was a beautiful looking pup that grew into a beautiful looking dog – not too big or too heavy who was named Karl after the play-pen pet.

From the first he was nervous: inclined to hide behind the sofa and peep out from behind chairs or under the bed. I expected there to be a measure of nervousness at first as he missed the company of the other members of the litter but his attitude did not appear to be improving with time. He was relatively happy in the house so long as there were no visitors. However, it worried me when he continued to hide under the bed or the sofa rather than relax by the fire or in his basket.

As I lived on the edge of the town I was able to take him for walks in the open countryside where he behaved well learning to come when called and to obey essential commands. However, he resented anyone approaching us and developed a habit of bouncing around me, barking his hair raised his tail whipping from side to side. With time I had hoped to train him out of this threatening and aggressive looking behaviour but it became worse and, as he grew, it became more frightening. There was never any question of him attacking or frightening me: rather it was a case of him protecting me and warning off strangers.

I worked with him for a year and a half. During that time all my family supported me, welcoming Karl but with increasing reservations about his future. They felt that the possibility of him attacking someone was increasing rather than deceasing, we were worried that he might attack our baby son. I loved Karl but could not ignore what was being said by my extended family, all of whom were dog lovers. At last I agreed that we should take Karl to a local expert in the Alsatian world for advice in the hope that he could direct us in training that would solve the problem. I agreed to accept what the expert recommended.

I kept my word. We were told that in the opinion of the expert Karl would never pose a threat to me – he was my dog and loyal to me – but there was a very real threat of him attacking someone else. The advice was that he should be put down. I kept my word.

Spud

My Family Dog

My son was born before another dog was found so he grew up with the next dog. This dog was also a mongrel, not unlike Scamp in size and shape though he had a longer tail. My son was only a few months old and we had just moved into a new house that was not quite complete when we purchased the pup. Again there was much debate over the name.

The lounge of the house was raised above ground level and the builder, as a temporary measure, had left a small hole in the floor so that he could make adjustments to the wiring that was attached to the joists.

We were living on bare floorboards partly because we did not have the money for carpets and partly because carpets would not be fitted till the pup learned to do 'his business' outside. The very first night the fire was lit and the new pup was allowed into the sparsely furnished lounge. He tore round the room and promptly fell down the hole. There was a good four-foot drop under the floor and the hole was the only way either in or out. I approached the hole, frantically trying to imagine how we might reach our pup and rescue him only to find that his leg had caught in one of the wires. He was hanging just below the floor within easy reach.

So he was named. Spud was deemed a very appropriate name for an animal silly enough to fall down a hole but lucky enough to survive.

My son proved to be as much of an adventurer as the dog. From an early age as a toddler he took to nocturnal wanderings around the house. These adventures often involved noise that awakened the whole household and on one occasion the residents of the adjoining bungalow.

We had been wakened by a noise that we could not place and, unable to identify the source, we experienced a period of true terror before we managed to shine some light on the matter. Light revealed a small person in small pyjamas waving a huge piece of tin foil while standing grinning in the bedroom doorway beside a tail wagging Spud.

The second episode was even more terrifying. We were awakened by an ear-shattering booming noise. The whole house seemed to be vibrating. This time the light revealed nothing so, while the noise continued, we tip toed to the main living room from whence that noise appeared to be coming. And there he was again, small person in small pyjamas hanging out of our 'top of the range' record player dropping the stylus on the revolving turntable. And there was Spud standing beside him, his happy, smiling, tail-wagging accomplice.

His third adventure involved no noise at all. I headed to the kitchen first thing one morning to discover that all of the painted cupboard doors at low level and some parts of the floor had been brushed with black shoe polish. Small person in small pyjamas had been silently busy and had equally silently returned to bed. Like an equally silent and invisible Spud. No amount of scrubbing removed the purple stain left by the polish.

There were times of peace and quiet and these were valued when I was working. Arriving home from school coincided with a TV programme about 'Skippy The Bush Kangaroo'. So, the routine was: into the house; place little son on the floor in front of the TV; turn it on; small person sat mesmerised while the programme lasted and I had peace to prepare the dinner. However, when Skippy had rescued everyone and the programme came to an end with the song *about Skippy Skippy The Bush Kangaroo* a howl went up followed by a heart broken wail of *'Come back Skippy. Come back Skippy, Come back Skippy'*. Spud retired to his basket when the howl went up.

Spud was a wonderful family dog – good with children and full of fun. He developed a great talent for retrieving and would chase and return anything that could be thrown – a ball, a stick, a slipper, a sock, a toy, and if all else failed, a stone. His energy seemed boundless and he was prepared to fetch for much longer than most were prepared to throw. On the odd occasion when he did tire he would flop down to do a bit of panting and chewing till he was ready to resume the game.

During Spud's early years we lived in a house just outside the town. The route into town lay along a golf course where Spud discovered golf balls. As I walked into town he trotted along the course popping out to drop a golf ball in front of the pram every now and then. This might have been very embarrassing had he chewed them or had anyone been actually playing at the time. He never touched a ball that was in play and never chewed any golf ball so I could return with four or five, sometimes quite valuable, golf balls.

You can imagine how popular this made him with the golfing members of the family. He was taken on walks along the course when all golfers had quit for the day and even, on occasion, accompanied family members on informal golfing outings so no-one ever lost a ball.

This was the first dog that demonstrated the ability to train humans. For him a walk was not complete without some fetching. We played along but there is only so much throwing a person would do. When that point was reached Spud had a short rest and then set about his 'train the human' routine.

He would select a stick, a ball, or stone, drop it in front of any one standing idly near to hand. He'd then crouch down and shuffle back with his bottom up in the air, his ears pricked, tail wagging, his tongue lolling and his head cocked to one side. He knew that most humans were hard to train. He did not expect them to respond first time so he quickly picked up the missile and dropped it nearer the pupil to repeat his bottom, ears, tail and head manoeuvre. Most humans got the message after the third lesson. By then Spud's new pupil was trained to throw and the fun could begin.

Over time he became so adept at judging the throw that he was sometimes at the arrival point to catch the ball before it hit the ground or caught it on the first bounce. As a result we were tempted to tease him by dropping the ball behind us before continuing on the dummy throw. When Spud arrived at the place where he **knew** the ball should land he COULDN'T BELIEVE IT. Searching in the sky in case there was a delayed arrival he then made a quick search of the ground before running back to the thrower. It might have been possible to fool him once or twice but after that he hovered till he was quite sure where the ball was going – he was no dummy!

There was one occasion where his talent nearly cost him his life. He was playing 'throw and fetch' with my son and a couple of his friends when he caught the stick before it landed point first down his throat. He started to choke. One of the boys had the presence of mind to run and pull out the stick. Fortunately no serious damage had occurred but it ended the fun for that day. Many years passed before I heard this story!

While he loved to fetch when he was outdoors he would wrestle endlessly indoors. He had a rubber ring that would be bounced on a knee till the human took it in hand. Then Spud would brace his front legs, and pull hard with growling grunts accompanying each tug. He wagged a delighted tail if the opposition obliged with growling grunts in return. Even more delighted if the opposition got down on hands and knees to growl.

Spud was a happy confident dog. However, there was one date each year when he was truly and utterly miserable – Hallowe'en. At that time fireworks were readily available. It was common for families to hold firework parties in their back gardens. When the night arrived and the noise started Spud turned into a shivering, panting, dribbling, whining bundle that cowered behind a sofa, beneath a bed, under a chair or in a corner and nothing we could do relieved his terror.

We endured that for two years in the hope that he would eventually become used to the noise when, in fact, things only got worse. We reached the point when we realised that something had to be done and made an approach to our vet who supplied us with pills that acted as a sedative. Spud slept through every Hallowe'en after that.

Though Spud was free to wander as dogs were allowed to do, for the most part, in those days, he seldom strayed very far from home unless it was to visit my parents where he stayed while I was at work. From time to time Spud discovered a lady friend. When that happened he was prepared to travel the length of the town and remain endlessly constant, attentive and hopeful, day and night, ignoring any other suitors that might be in attendance. We usually located the lady friend and brought our love sick dog home where he was confined till it was safe to let him out.

Spud had an amazing ability to jump and climb. A six foot wall represented no problem to him. One spring Spud discovered a lady friend that was kept at night in a shed in her owner's back yard. The shed had originally been a coal-store but had been converted into a kennel. Though the door fitted well it had a space of around eighteen inches at the top to let in light and help keep the air fresh. The owner of the dog shut her in each night and brought her into the house during the day. It worked well until one morning when he opened the door and Spud strolled out past him. Love had found a way!

Spud had a long, happy life. In the end when the vet was no longer able to do anything for kidney failure and he was in great distress and pain I am not sure who had the more difficult job – me in tears trying to console children who could not be consoled or the husband who had to take Spud on his final journey.

ROY

A Dog a Bit Cat Like

Our first dog was called Scamp. After Scamp my parents were loathe to have another dog. I think they wanted the freedom to come and go as they liked without having to place the dog before any journey could be undertaken. However, with the arrival of Spud in my house they rediscovered the joy a dog could add to their lives as I arrived at their home one day to find them playing with a new pup. There was no debate over the naming of this animal. He had already been named Roy. Roy was a short haired terrier – white with a black head. He was small. In no time at all he became Wee Roy.

Wee Roy was a lively dog, not very clever but good with children and got on with Spud. The two dogs would play their favourite game of 'tug the floor cloth', one at either end pulling hard and growling. Wee Roy was not as interested in retrieving but did not like to see Spud have the fun all to himself so he would chase the ball to take it away from Spud but had no interest at all in returning it to the bowler.

Wee Roy was cat-like in character, a bit aloof and independent. He was not one to cuddle up if allowed on the sofa though he would lie close to warm up if the room was chilly. He really did not like to be cold. While still quite young found that if he lay on top of the dining room table just under the window the sun warmed him up beautifully. That was his afternoon post while in the evening he lay along the back of the sofa in the lounge to make the most of the evening sunshine. Both locations had the added bonus that he could keep an eye on all the comings and goings outside. In the evening when the fire was lit he lay on the hearth as close to the heat as possible – sometimes so close, in fact, that he had to be pulled away to avoid him going up in smoke!.

As was the custom with all dogs that we had over the years Wee Roy was let out at bedtime long enough to 'do his business'. In the cold weather this was a problem for Wee Roy. Being ushered out into a cold dark garden from a warm house made no sense to him and, in the early days, he refused to go so my father had to carry him out, dump him in the garden, run in and shut the door before Wee Roy could nip back in. As my father had no enthusiasm for these cold nocturnal jaunts either he developed a routine that saved him the trouble. Come bed-time he called Wee Roy and set off to run through the house to the back door making growling noises and shouting 'Where is that cat Roy? Get those birds' by the time the back door was reached Wee Roy was barking and frantic to dash out to catch any cat or bird that might be lurking in *his* garden. It worked every time! It was assumed that, by the time he came in, he had 'done his business'.

My mother had been brought up on a farm and always managed to have a vegetable garden attached to any house in which she lived. She eventually prevailed on my father to provide a green house. A bit of a DIY person he decided to build a lean-to greenhouse himself at the back of the house off the kitchen. Over one spring and summer, my father laid down the foundations, built the low walls before installing the wooden framework that would support the glazing. This work was completed at weekends and in the evenings during the better weather when the days were long but with the arrival of winter all work ceased.

The following spring glass was ordered, my father enlisted friends to help and one day the green house was glazed. My father was proud of his handiwork. My mother was delighted with her greenhouse.

That evening at bedtime when my father had completed his growling and 'get those birds' routine he opened the kitchen door and Wee Roy charged straight out to jump over the green house wall, over the garden wall into the field behind the house.

No one had told him about the glass.

There was an almighty crash.

We ran towards the greenhouse. Was Wee Roy impaled on the broken glass, was he lying cut to ribbons in the greenhouse, was he outside bleeding to death? One section of glass was in bits and there was no sign of Wee Roy in the greenhouse. There was so sign of him in the garden. Was he dead in the field? Just as my father turned to fetch his torch to look for Wee Roy he bounced up on the garden wall and jumped down into the garden wagging his tail. There was not a mark on him. He had been travelling so quickly that he sailed right through the glass unharmed.

A stone's throw from my parents' house a neighbour kept hens in his back garden. There was a henhouse inside a fair-sized run that was fenced off with chicken wire. The fence was secure enough to keep the hens in but, as we found out when the owner of the hens came calling, not robust enough to keep Wee Roy out. Wee Roy had managed to get in, cause havoc amongst the chicken community without actually killing any, and get back out again. Apologies were made, assurances given and the chicken man departed. Some discussion followed where it was agreed that if it happened again serious consideration would have to be given to Wee Roy's future. I knew what that meant!

When my parents went on holiday a couple of months later I was left in charge of Wee Roy. Early one afternoon a loud knocking on the door heralded the arrival of a furious chicken man. Wee Roy had killed one of his hens. I knew that something had to be done. If Wee Roy had enjoyed chasing a hen to death once it stood to reason that he would repeat the entertainment. I assured the chicken man that I would pay for the dead hen provided he brought the corpse to me. He agreed, so the chicken was handed over and I paid the price.

Then I set about teaching Wee Roy that chickens were no fun at all either dead or alive. Holding him by the collar and pressing the dead chicken up against his nose I slapped him on his rear end whilst telling him that

good dogs did not chase chickens

and that he must stay away from them in future. He took his punishment like a man and never looked at another chicken as long as he lived.

Kelly

I Am Outvoted

After Spud I wanted no more dogs. It was my time to be outvoted and outnumbered. My family fully intended to have another dog. I could either help to pick it or accept their choice so, as graciously as my father before me had surrendered, I went along with them.

Our new pup came from a farm and this time was a mongrel bitch with more than a little of the Labrador in her ancestry. She had been born and had remained in one of the farm outbuildings. When we first met her, she had never been in a house. She showed signs of distress at being removed from her mother and the remainder of the litter so the journey to our house in a car was the last straw. She panted and shivered till she threw up just before we reached our destination. Travelling was always to prove difficult for her but we learned that if the journey was broken up with frequent comfort stops we avoided the mess. She was black with white feet. The children selected the name Kelly.

Once again we had found a good family dog though there was a little stubborn streak in her in that, unlike most dogs, she was not always out to please.

We had always had dogs. We certainly did not wish to have pups however cute they might be so Kelly was taken to the family vet as one of her first outings. She informed us that Kelly would have to come into season once before the small operation, that would ensure that no pups appeared, could be undertaken. We were instructed to keep Kelly in when that happened. We followed instructions. The back garden was enclosed by fence and hedge so she was safe there - no dog could get in, she could not get out until day three, when I saw Kelly galloping off over the golf course accompanied by another dog.

Of course, she came back but we had to assume that the damage had been done so it was straight to the vet for an injection. Then back home to find out how she escaped. The route was quickly located. She had dug under the hedge to run through the neighbouring garden to the golf course –a mind of her own!

Shortly after we acquired Kelly we moved to a house beside a golf course. Kelly's bed was in the snug with patio doors opening out to the garden with the course just over the back wall. It was the room most used by the family as it was cosy with a sofa and a couple of easy chairs, next to the kitchen and handy for allowing Kelly to come and go.

In no time it became obvious that, though she always used her bed during the day, she favoured the sofa at night after we had retired. There was no easy way of stopping this so at night I draped a rug over the sofa, inviting her up. She had me trained and that was the way it remained.

Kelly had been easy to house train and very soon learned to bark to demand to be let out even during the night. The first winter in the new house was unusually cold. One night she looked so forlorn as we went to bed that I fetched another rug and tucked it in round her. She loved it! Snug as a bug with her wee black nose peeping out. About a week later I was wakened by Kelly barking, so hurried along to the snug to let her out. I slid open the patio door, stood aside to let her past but she just stood there looking at me. I pointed to the garden and told her to go but to no avail. Then I noticed that her eyes were drifting between me and the sofa. Could it be..........? I patted the sofa, she needed no other invitation. Up she jumped, snuggled down and sighed deeply when I tucked the rug round her. What dog owner wants to get out of bed in the cold to tuck a dog in but sometimes she did need to go out and she always kept me guessing.

Our next door neighbours were encouraged to get a dog when we moved in and they saw what a dog contributed to a family. Their Labrador, named Chaucer, was a house pet during the day but was housed in a kennel inside a run during the night or when they were at work. Both dogs were welcome in both houses.

One night Kelly did not return when she was let out. When half an hour had passed without any sign I went out to look for her. I called and whistled to no avail. I was extremely worried because it was most unlike her to spend much time outside at night in the cold weather. When she was missing for nearly an hour I found a torch, climbed on to the wall and flashed it out over the golf course and across the neighbouring back gardens. As the light swept over the garden next door I saw two pairs of red eyes gazing at me. I called but the eyes never moved. I tip toed round to the next garden and there was Kelly shut in the run with Chaucer. She had gone visiting before Chaucer was put to bed and had been shut in.

Though Kelly never enjoyed retrieving in the same way as Spud had done, nevertheless, she loved to select a stick and carry it along in her mouth. Sometimes the stick was brought the whole way home, sometimes not, depending on what diversions occurred. One day on the return leg of our walk we came upon a six-foot-long pole that Kelly decided was her 'must have' take-home trophy. It took a couple of attempts for her to find the balance point before she pranced off with three feet of pole sticking out on either side of her jaws much to the amusement of other dog walkers.

As we approached the house I stopped a second for a quick word with a neighbour as Kelly went ahead with her trophy, so as I rounded the corner of the house I was just in time to see Kelly made the rather painful discovery that, even when carried proudly by a very clever black dog, a six foot pole does not easily pass through a four foot doorway.

Chaucer

And Dogs That Came Calling

Though Chaucer belonged to our next-door neighbour he spent a lot of time with me and my family. When our neighbours were at work he joined us and was known to have accompanied us on holiday when his owners travelled abroad. He was a big very handsome black Labrador that had royal connections.

Chaucer was a very friendly animal who came visiting with the most enthusiastic tail ever seen. His tail was not long but it was substantial and was whipped fiercely from side to side when he greeted us. In time his tail had to be controlled. One afternoon he came calling. When he was admitted he began his tail wagging greeting. We suddenly realised that some sort of specks were flying through the air and before we had identified them the chairs, the walls and the curtains were smattered with these specks. Chaucer kept waging till it dawned on us that the smatters were tiny drops of blood coming from poor Chaucer's tail – he had whipped it so hard from side to side that he had damaged it on a hard surface. With care it did heal but on future visits we had to capture Chaucer's tail on arrival and calm his enthusiastic greeting.

On one occasion when Chaucer's owners were going away for two weeks we were delighted to have him stay with us. Our neighbours were not due to depart till around twelve o'clock but Chaucer was left in with us mid-morning along with his bed and bowls. One thing stroked off the list of things to do before departure!

At lunch time I put a small meal in each dog's bowl and called them. They were both rather fond of their food. Kelly came trotting along to gobble up her lunch but there was no sign of Chaucer. I went out whistled and called but there was neither sight nor sound of him. I was puzzled as it was not like him to wander, particularly near mealtimes. I knew he wouldn't have wandered off but the fact remained that he had disappeared. All rooms in the house were examined along with the surrounding gardens but no trace of him was found. He was a valuable dog. We started to wonder if he had been snatched for breeding purposes. What on earth were we to tell the owners on their return – that their precious pet had gone missing before they had even left the country?

In desperation we looked again in all the places we had searched before. Maybe we had missed him first time round. I went to have a second look in his outdoor run. As I passed the kitchen window happened to glance in and saw a movement. I stepped back and peered through the window. There he was smiling at me, wagging his tail. We had found him.

Our relief was short lived. I had no key. How were we to get him out? By this time many of the neighbours were involved. Amid all the suggestions someone mentioned the police. With no better ideas forthcoming and with little hope of it being a solution we phoned the local police station.

It must have been a crime free day as two policemen arrived shortly after we made the call. They, in their wisdom, confirmed that, indeed there was a dog shut in the neighbour's kitchen and suggested that the key holder should open the door and release the dog. We pointed out that if a key had been available we would not have called them in the first place. They then voiced the opinion that the dog could stay there till the owners returned. We reminded them that the owners were away for two weeks and no-one could leave an animal locked up for that length of time. The two policemen got into a huddle to discuss possibilities and requested that I make a cup of tea.

Before the kettle boiled the two police and Chaucer were at my side. To this day I don't know how the miracle was worked. Chaucer was safe, the neighbouring house was secure, the policemen had a cup of tea and departed to solve their next crime!

At that time I walked regularly sometimes twice a day always taking Kelly and Chaucer with me. Other dogs noticed my comings and goings and two dogs living nearby started to join me. So I could set out with three dogs and find myself with four or five inside a couple of minutes.

One of these rascals joined me as we walked past his house, accompanied us on the walk and returned to his owner on the way back. The other, Bonny by name and by nature, often arrived at our house anticipating the walk long before 'walk time', accompanied us on our way and remained till tea time when her owner returned from work.

On the walk I had one road to cross and my obedient troupe always remained on the footpath till I gave the command when they trotted to the other side. There never was any aggression either amongst them or towards any other dogs we would meet nor any chasing motorbikes!

In those days we owned a mobile home based on a caravan park in a small Donegal village beside the golf course and a stone throw from the beach. From Easter till Halloween many week-ends, and most of the summer months, were spent there – another place where children and dogs were free to wander.

A local family who spent all week-ends and all of the summer months at the park had a van almost beside us. They had a delightful yellow Labrador called Alana. The children quickly made friends and, with them going back and forth between the vans, it was not long before their dog started to visit. She very soon realised that I walked the length of the beach every day and she was free to accompany me. She also loved to fetch but for her if the ball went into the sea that was an added bonus. Unless a member of her family appeared she stayed with me the whole way there and back but if, on the homeward leg, we met anyone she knew who was setting out she promptly deserted me to join the new walking group.

Though she never saw us at all over the winter months she remembered us from year to year. Every time when we arrived she was with us before we had time to unpack the car wagging her tail furiously and giving us a royal welcome. She remained a part of our summers for five years.

Then one Easter we arrived but encountered no doggy welcome. We were told that she had disappeared from her home during the winter and despite all the efforts of the family was never found. There had been much speculation over what might have happened. It was thought that she had been stolen for breeding. For years after I never passed a yellow dog wandering alone without slowing down and peering in the hope of catching a glimpse of a yellow Labrador that would prove to be Alana.

There is one dog – one that I never met, who never came calling, whose name and breed I never knew, yet is one that I will always remember.

We were holidaying in Paris staying with relations who took us out sightseeing each day. One of the highlights of these trips was a cruise along the Seine. It was a beautiful day allowing us to travel smoothly along the river taking in the places of interest along the way. We had just passed under one of the many bridges and were approaching another when I saw a dog jump on to the wall of the bridge. To my horror, it flew right over, all four legs scrambling desperately for ground that was not there falling straight down into the water. It disappeared beneath the surface.

Others on our boat had noticed what had happened so there was a chorus of cries and gasps as we waited.......... the dog surfaced........ there was a communal sigh of relief.

It started to swim. There were many parts of the bank where it would have been possible for a dog to scramble out but equally as many where steep banks would render that impossible. The dog was swimming towards a gently sloping bank nearest to where it had fallen in and nearing our boat.

All traffic on the river had halted. Passengers in the boats were watching, the banks were crowded, the bridge was packed with people all willing the dog on. It drew near our boat so that crew members reached out to it in the hope that it would come near enough for them to drag it out. We held our breath. I noticed that a woman near me was standing, eyes closed, hands clasped under her chin and muttering. It was a low voice spoken in a foreign language so that it was not till she dropped her hands to cross herself that it dawned on me that she was praying for the dog.

Then, without warning, the dog paddled round to commence swimming away from us out towards the middle of the river. Boats were still, people silent as we watched. We watched as the dog swam away from us towards the distant bank. We watched as the little head became smaller and smaller. We watched as if the head would disappear if we took our eyes off it. That swim seemed to last forever and then......... the little head disappeared. A moan went up from the passengers in our boat. My lip trembled. The man beside me, suddenly realising that he had binoculars hanging from a strap round his neck pressed them to his eyes.

"It's OK" he shouted. "It's OK It's safe. It's out"

A burst of clapping and cheering went up as the dog shook itself on the bank at the other side. It had done what seemed impossible. It was safe. The river, that had held its breath for an unknown dog, became alive again.

Lady

The Dog Who Found Us

One winter evening just as it was starting to get dark I noticed a black dog out on the golf course behind our house. It was snowing and the dog was cowering among the long grass in the lee of a low hill that offered a measure of shelter from the biting northerly wind. I realized that I had seen that black dog on a couple of occasions on the previous day and wondered if it could possibly be a stray.

The situation was discussed by the members of the family. It was decided that we should try to coax the dog into the garage where it could be kept safe, fed and warm till the next day when we would set about finding the owner. So, I donned my coat and hood, collected some doggy treats, climbed over the wall and set about enticing the shivering animal through the back door of the garage. Try as I might there was no way that the dog would enter. She allowed me to approach her, she took treats that were offered, but would not come near the garage door.

I spent some time with her and at last came to the conclusion that the only other alternative was to try to tempt her into the house. I also came to the conclusion that if **I** issued the invitation and it proved to be a disaster I would carry all the blame. So I slowly returned to the patio doors went in and shut them, informing the family that I had done all I could and the dog would just have to stay out. As I finished speaking the little wet, bedraggled, miserable shivering dog appeared in the snow outside the door just as I guessed she would. It was too much for the family. With one voice they declared that she should come in. And thus it was!

We did all that we could to find an owner: contacted the police, approached the local vet, spoke to all the dog walkers and spread the word every possible way but no-one came forward. Meantime the dog stayed with us, was taken to the vet for a health check was fed and walked along with Kelly and Chaucer. Her gentle, shy, obedient and slightly nervous nature earned the name Lady. So a second set of dog bowls and another dog bed were added and Lady became ours.

Lady was a timid, shy dog however the others accepted her without question. Our favourite walk was through the sand hills but it was a very long time before she would walk ahead of me or trot along to either side of the path bouncing and sniffing with the other dogs. She opted to walk close to heel. It was a day of great joy when I realised that she was not at my heels but sniffing, making short sorties to left and right. I knew then that she was happy, secure and her sad past was forgotten.

Sometimes our walk would take us along the bank of the river at a point just before it entered the sea. Occasionally we would spot a seal swimming along popping its head up to peer around before diving again. Chaucer and Kelly found this fascinating and would stand on the bank staring at the seal as it appeared and disappeared. The seal seemed to have the same fascination for the dogs as each time its little black head surfaced, he was looking in our direction. This entertainment could last for up to half an hour before he departed. I always wondered what they thought of each other.

When Lady had been with us for several weeks we took her to the vet for a follow up check. I was very pleased with the progress Lady had made: she looked well, seemed content and had put on some weight. I mentioned this to the vet and, to my surprise, she burst out laughing. 'Of course she has' she said. 'She's pregnant.'

I knew plenty about how to manage dogs but on the subject of animal midwifery I had no knowledge at all. So, while Lady quietly expanded, we studied books on the delivery of pups, the management of expectant dogs and made decisions on where the birth was to take place. We were warned that the expectant mother, when the time came, was liable to seek out a hiding place in which to deliver her pups. So, the kitchen was to become the maternity ward and we were to keep a close eye on her near the time.

Though we approached the happy event with some trepidation we might not have worried because, when the time came, Lady, in typical lady-like manner, delivered nine beautiful healthy pups in the kitchen with minimal help from the humans. She was distressed just before and during the delivery of her first born but thereafter the pups appeared at regular intervals three black Labradors, three yellow and finally three black.

She was an ideal mother attending to the pups when needed and leaving them sleeping when they were content. One painful duty remained. The vet advised that Lady simply could not manage nine pups and suggested that, if any pups were to be kept, there should be a minimum of two and a maximum of four. We went for the four – two yellow and two black - a dog and a bitch of each.

I could take no part with either the selection or removal process: it was left to the family. However, I knew that the right decision had been made when it became obvious that Lady was much more content with her four pups than she had been with the nine.

For the first few weeks the doggy family remained fenced in the utility end of the kitchen by a line of boxes. Each morning, first thing, I had the unpleasant but very necessary job of cleaning and disinfecting the area of the kitchen they occupied. Meantime we prepared the garage, constructing a run outside so pups and Lady could come and go safely. When the pups were old enough and sufficiently developed, they were moved to the garage and my disinfecting duties ended. The fencing was high enough to keep pups in but low enough to let Lady jump in and out and they all thrived.

Our next big hurdle was that of finding suitable homes for the pups. In that we were lucky, as friends and neighbours expressed interest so that in no time three were promised and, in due course, taken to their new homes. Not so easy for the fourth.

One day I received a phone call from an unknown man expressing interest in the last pup. He agreed to come along for what he called a look before making a final commitment and what I viewed as an interview. He reacted well to the pup but in the course of conversation boasted that he had a well-paid job working nine to five lived alone so the pup would be well provided for. A bit of quick thinking was needed. I certainly did not intend to hand over the pup to a well-meaning but absentee owner. The pup was only going where I knew that it would be cherished night and day. I looked the young man in the eye and told him that the pup was being held for a week for another person but that if that placing failed I would get in touch with him. We did, of course, find a very suitable home for the last pup in the end.

We had one more little surprise. The yellow dog went to a family who lived nearby while the black dog was homed in another town and neither family knew the other yet both dogs were named Sam.

Kelly had a long life. It is strange, but before Kelly it never occurred to me to wonder what happened to the body of a dog when it was put down. When our vet once again advised that she could do no more to cure or relieve Kelly's suffering I knew that she had to be buried in our garden and she was.

We never knew how old Lady was. When her time came she also was buried in the garden.

I had never heard her bark.

Brothers and sisters I bid you beware
Of giving your heart to a dog to tear

"The Power of the Dog"
Rudyard Kipling

Scamp

Spud

Wee Roy

Kelly

Lady

Bonny

Chaucer

Alana

Karl

Two of the many that crossed my path enriching my life

ABOUT THE AUTHOR

Yvonne Hamilton is a retired primary school teacher living in the seaside town of Portstewart Northern Ireland. She has been a member of the North Coast Writers for 2 years. She started to write when she had to retire from a small amateur orchestra when poor night vision made it unsafe for her to travel to rehearsals. That gave her the time – her dogs gave inspiration

Printed in Great Britain
by Amazon

21373729R00041